I Can BE

by Christine Sumner
Illustrated by Kirk Salopek

Dedicated to Quinton, W.J., and Jacob

Special thanks to the Greensburg Writers Group, Judith Gallagher, and Ruth Rittenhouse for their support.

Q & J Bird Press, LLC
141 Morey Place
Greensburg, PA 15601
www.qandjbirdpress.com

ISBN 13:978-0-615-16566-0

It is recommended that you consult a physician before you begin any of the movements or practices described in *I Can Be*. The publisher, the author, and the illustrator cannot accept responsibility for any injuries or damages that may occur from the proper or improper use of information provided in this book.

Printed and bound in the United States

I can
CAW
like a
crow.

I
can
BUZZ
like a
bee.

I
can
GROW
just as
tall

as
the
very
tallest tree.

I can HISS
like a snake.

I can JUMP like a frog.

I can LOOK at my paws like a downward-facing dog.

I can ARCH like a cat.

I can HUG

like a bear.

I can FLY
like a butterfly flitting through the air.

I
can
BEND.

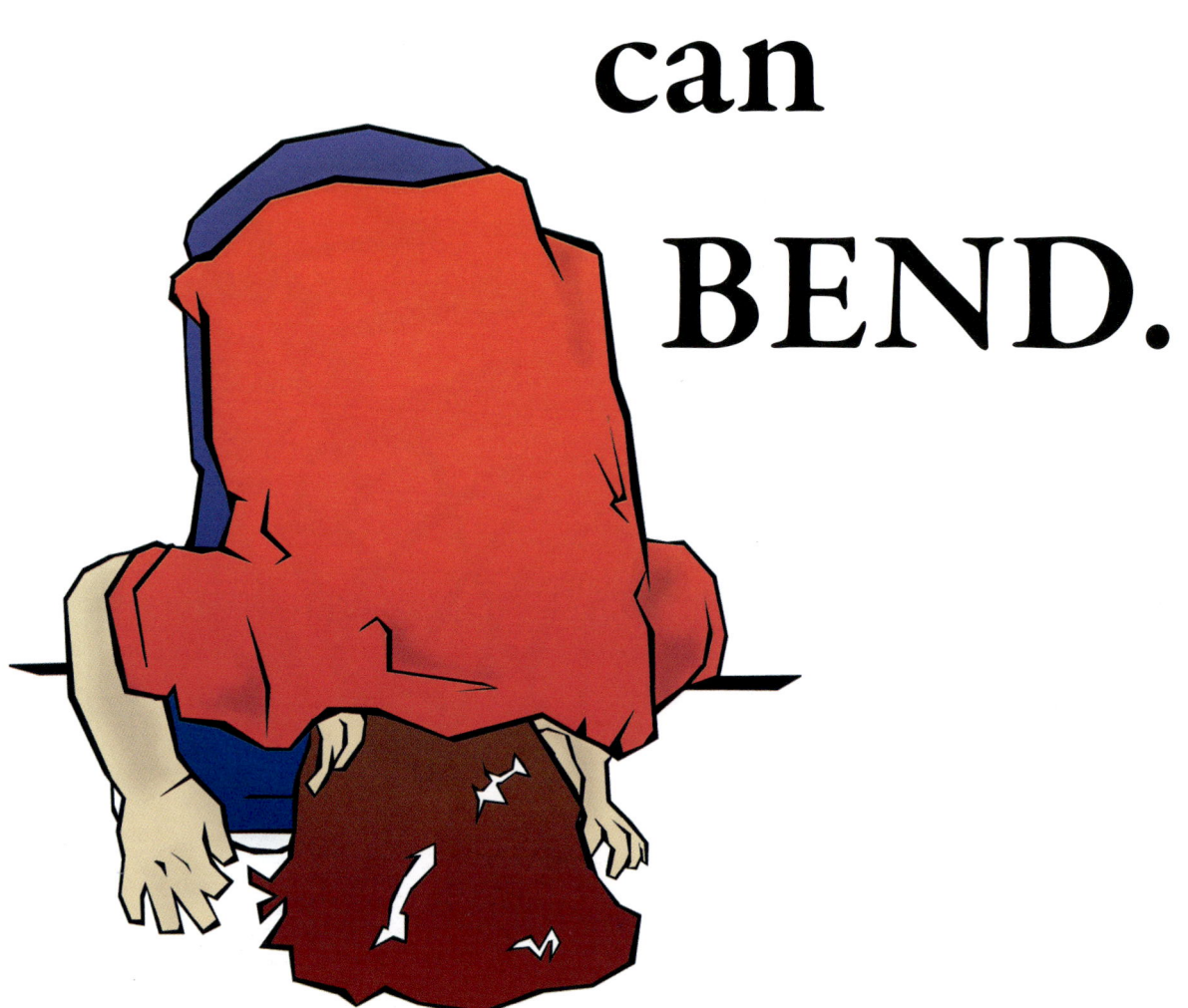

I
can
STRETCH.

I can

BALANCE.

I can BE.

That's what makes me special.

That's
what
makes
me

ME!

Instructions for Caregivers

Below are more detailed instructions to perform each yoga pose with your child. Remember, the pose does not have to be perfect! Ask your child to become the animal, observe her or his interpretation of the pose, and offer gentle guidance and instruction. Don't forget to breathe!

Crow Pose
Stand up straight, inhale, and lift your arms out to shoulder height. Gently begin to flap your arms up and down like a crow stretching its wings. Let out a few caws and you are doing the crow!

Bee Pose
With your elbows bent, place the back of your fingers just below your armpits. Move your arms forward and backward. Fly around the room like a bee moving from flower to flower and allow a buzzing sound to resound. Now you are buzzing like a bee!

Tree Pose
Stand upright with your feet slightly apart. Look straight ahead and focus your gaze on the horizon. Place your right foot on your inner left calf or thigh. Place hands at heart center in a prayer position. Take a big breath in, with your mouth closed, and imagine that you are becoming a tree by stretching your arms and leaves up to the sky. As you breathe out, exit the pose by releasing your hands down and lowering your leg. Repeat on the opposite side.

Snake Pose
Lie on your belly with your forehead on the floor. Place your hands on the floor at the sides of your chest. Hold your elbows tight along the sides of your body. Firm the muscles of your legs and backside. On the in breath, gently lift up your torso like a long snake and hiss! Keep your neck long and set your gaze at the floor below you. Come down slowly on the out breath.

Frog Pose
Come to a squatting position. To jump like a frog, place your hands on the floor along the sides of your feet, press your hands into the ground, and leap high up into the sky! Don't forget to ribbit!

Downward-facing Dog
Come to the floor on your hands and knees. Spread your fingers. Turn your toes under and press your hands into the ground. Exhale and begin to lift your knees, hips, and backside up to the sky. Allow your legs to straighten and your heels to come toward the ground. Your heels do not need to touch the ground! Keep your head between your upper arms and remain in the pose for a few breaths. To exit the pose, exhale and carefully come back to your hands and knees. Bow-wow!

Cat Pose
Remain on your hands and knees. As you breathe out, bring your chin toward your chest and arch your back toward the sky like a Halloween cat. Inhale and return to your starting position. Meow!

Bear Pose

This pose is easy and fun! Give your loved one a big hug and a growl. If practicing by yourself, place your hands on your opposite shoulders and give yourself a big squeeze! Grrrh!

Butterfly Pose

Sit and place the bottoms of your feet together. Hold onto your ankles and bring your heels close to your body. Cup your hands around the tops of your feet and sit up tall. On the in breath, bring your knees up toward the sky. On the out breath, lower your knees toward the ground. Continue inhaling your knees up and exhaling them down. Imagine that your legs are the wings of a butterfly and fly to the nearest cloud!

Standing Forward Bend

Stand straight with your feet slightly apart. Take a big breath in with your mouth closed. On the out breath, move into a forward bend by folding forward from the hips and touch your toes. Lower the crown of your head toward the ground. Hold for a few breaths. Exit the pose by performing the next stretch.

Overhead Stretch

From the forward bend position, bend your knees. As you breathe in, bring your arms out to your sides and come to a standing position with a strong back. Keep breathing while you stretch your arms over your head. Release your arms as you breathe out.

Balance (Airplane)

Stand and find a spot on the floor ahead of you to focus your attention. Balance on your left foot and spread your arms out to the side as you lift your right leg into the air behind you. Remember to breathe and hold the position for a few breaths. To exit the pose, exhale and lower your leg and arms and return to standing. *For a less challenging balancing pose, you can balance on one foot and place your arms out to your sides at shoulder height.*

Be (Meditation)

Meditation has untold benefits for the body, mind, and spirit. By simply *being,* we can connect to the true happiness and light that is within each of us! Start by practicing for a few minutes every day. Increase your practice time as you grow more experienced.

To begin, sit cross-legged on the floor with a pillow under your backside. Lift your spine up and relax your shoulders down. Level your head over your shoulders. Place your hands on your thighs with your palms facing either up or down. Close your eyes and begin to feel your breath move in and out of your body. Observe your thoughts as they come and go, without judgment. Move into meditation by continuing to focus on your breath or begin to mentally repeat any word, phrase, or prayer that brings you joy. *Tip: Have the child assume a comfortable position with closed eyes and say, "hum." They can continue humming until they need to take a breath and then start humming again.*